Cybercrime Protection Book
For Your Family & Finances

Minimize Your Exposure To Cybercrime Using These Essential Steps

Cybercrime is on track to become a six trillion dollar problem by 2021. After the Equifax breach, cybercrime advisors are alerting citizens that they should *assume* their personal information is in the hands of cyber criminals.

In this essential guide, Karen Freeman Worstell, breaks down the "what to do now" into 15 essential steps that will help to minimize your exposure.

It's more important than ever to begin and maintain good practices on a daily basis and to know what to do if you suspect your personal information has been misused. This handy guide shows you how.

For example:

- How to protect your social security accounts in case your number is exposed or misused.
- Detect the signs that indicate someone is trying to steal your bank account and take appropriate action.
- Simple steps to protect your online accounts from misuse.

Pick up a copy of this critical resource today and take action so you minimize your chances of becoming a cybercrime statistic.

Your Amazing Itty Bitty® Personal Data Protection Book

15 Keys to Minimize Your Exposure to Cybercrime Using These Essential Steps

Karen Worstell

Published by Itty Bitty® Publishing
A subsidiary of S & P Productions, Inc.

Printed in the United States of America

Itty Bitty® Publishing
311 Main Street, Suite D
El Segundo, CA 90245
(310) 640-8885

ISBN 978-0-9992211-9-8

Dedication

For all my cybersecurity colleagues over the last 30 years and for the decades to come, who warn and cajole industry leaders, design, operate, monitor, secure and patch technology, and who still have to write books to tell people how to recover from industry cybersecurity losses because the job is never done.

Keep up the good fight.

You all rock.

Stop by our Itty Bitty® website to find to interesting information regarding your personal data security.

www.IttyBittyPublishing.com

Or visit Karen Worstell at

www.karenworstell.com

Table of Contents

Introduction

In the wake of the Equifax breach in the summer of 2017, half of all American's most sensitive personal information affecting their financial well-being was in the hands of criminals after a single data breach. Since data breach record-keeping began in 2005, over 1 billion personal records have been breached through a variety of channels.

Data breaches are becoming so common it is safe to assume that your personal, sensitive data has been exposed. Identity theft is now the fastest growing crime in the United States. Identity theft is defined as the unlawful use or possession of Personal Identifiable Information (PII), financial identifying information or the financial device of another. PII may include your name, address, driver license number, Social Security number, date of birth or financial information such as your bank account or credit card information.

I wrote this book to give you the easy way to implement practices for protecting your identity from theft. This is a proactive and preventative approach. If you are already the victim of identity theft, there are additional steps you must take that are outlined at the following site:

https://www.identitytheft.gov/Info-Lost-or-Stolen.

You should do as many of these practices as you can, and here's why: cybercrime is still a crime of opportunity and convenience. The harder you make it, the less opportunity and the less convenient it is for a criminal to steal your data and drain your bank accounts.

Cybercrime is pervasive. There are never any guarantees; however, you can do a great deal now to limit the exposure of sensitive information and save yourself from lost time, headaches and possible harm to your financial reputation.

Step 1
Be Prepared – Assume the Worst

If you use online services, it is prudent to assume the worst and just assume that your information is exposed on the Dark Web or contained in data files owned by unauthorized individuals.

Get started now, and assemble the information you will need to move forward with protecting yourself and your family. Be proactive:

1. Get a complete inventory of all your financial accounts.
2. Know where your online data is – what are all the accounts you've set up online? Get the account and user logon information.
3. Get your "proof of identity" kit together.

Your Proof Of Identity Kit Contents

- Use one of those accordion-style folders you can get at any office supply for storing your records in an organized way.
- Keep these records protected. I recommend using a plastic tote to protect them from humidity and store in a secure location.
- Use a tabbed address book (I like the ones from Moleskine) and record all your online accounts with user ID and password.
- Get proof of identity information:
    - Social Security card with current name,
    - Passport if you have one,
    - Enhanced driver's license if available. An enhanced driver's license is available in a few states (WA, NY, VT, MI) and adds an additional layer of identity verification. It is also known as a "passport card."
    - Certified copy of birth certificate,
    - Proof of residence (a utility bill for example).

Step 2
Protect Your Bank Account with A PIN

One of the biggest concerns from data breaches is the ability for someone to impersonate you and to access accounts you have, such as your bank account.

To make sure that an impersonator cannot use stolen information like your SSN, address, date of birth and name to commit fraud against your bank accounts, set up a secret PIN for every account.

1. Go in person to your local bank branch, credit union or investment bank.
2. Tell them you wish to set up a secret PIN on your account.
3. Follow their guidance.

More About PINS

- Use a random set of numbers.
- Do not use '12345' or '11111' kinds of PINs.
- Do not use your address or phone.
- Do not use the same PIN for multiple accounts.

One way to pick a good PIN is to choose a word that you'll remember, and look up the numbers for it on a keypad. For example:

- WORLD is 96753
- ERASE is 37273

Step 3
Protect Your Credit History

There are smart steps that will reduce the exposure of your credit history to both hackers and inadvertent loss that is non-hacker related.

1. Don't apply for new credit if it's possible to avoid. If you know that you are not applying for new credit, then any alerts that appear on your credit report will be much easier to flag.
2. Put a freeze on your credit history account through Equifax, Experian, and TransUnion. No one will be able run an inquiry against your credit report without your permission.
3. If you are in the middle of a mortgage or business loan application, let your lender know what you've done, so that delays in your processing may be avoided. You may be asked to put a temporary lift on this freeze, so that those loans can complete processing.
4. Do not be a co-signer on a loan. It puts the quality of your credit history outside your control.

Limit Your Exposure

- Freeze your credit!
- Go to TransUnion.com and sign up for a "credit lock" that will freeze your credit at TransUnion, Experian, and Equifax for $19.95.
- Check your credit score and credit report.
- Cancel all unnecessary credit cards.
- Close accounts you no longer use, even if you don't have a credit card any longer.
- Keep track of all your activities: date you closed the account, and any documentation and correspondence.
- If you are concerned that you may be a victim of identity theft, but do not yet have a police report for it, you can place a temporary fraud alert on your credit file.

Step 4
Prove Your SSN is Yours

There is a weird type of identity theft that may be a lot more common than it appears and is hard to find. People can buy a valid SSN from the black market. It could be yours.

Get the data you need to prove that your SSN is yours and does not belong to the person who bought it.

1. Bring your certified birth certificate, your Social Security card and state-issued picture identification with you.
2. Go to your local Social Security office and tell them you need a "REPORT OF CONFIDENTIAL SOCIAL SECURITY BENEFIT INFORMATION" (Form SSA-2458) to prove you are the owner of your SSN.
3. It is a good idea to request multiple copies.

More Ways to Protect Your SSN

In addition, you may:

- Set up an online account at
  https://www.ssa.gov/myaccount/
- Ask for your Social Security Benefit
  report to be mailed to you regularly, or
  check it online as frequently as you want.
- Review your Social Security Benefit
  report regularly to ensure that nothing
  strange appears there.

For extra security, block all online access to your
social security data (this will also block you).

- Go to:
  https://secure.ssa.gov/acu/IPS_INTR/blo
  ckaccess
- If you choose to do this, you will need to
  go to the Social Security office in person
  with proof of your identification and SSN
  to get it unblocked.
- Do not do this for any account but your
  own. *Misrepresenting identity to the
  Social Security Administration is a
  federal crime.*

Step 5
Protect Your Driving Record

If you believe you are the victim of identity theft, or that someone is using your SSN, contact your state DMV Identity Theft division as soon as possible. You will need:

1. A police report from local law enforcement, or your Identity Theft affidavit from the FTC.
2. Official fingerprint cards with all 10 fingerprints. This can be obtained by contacting a fingerprinting agency like LiveScan.
3. Documents such as official birth certificate and documents showing your lawful presence.
4. A description (or police report) describing what has happened.

Updated information specific for your state can be found by searching online for "DMV Identity Theft."

More About Your Driving Records

- Felonies attached to your driving record
  and SSN are difficult, if not impossible to
  remove.
- Obtain an enhanced driver's license
  (requires fingerprints) if your state offers
  it.

Step 6
Use Multi-Factor Authentication

This is a big $64.00 phrase that basically means that you have extra layers of security to validate that your claimed identity is really you. Passwords are far too weak to be relied upon for online applications and services, so a second or even third form of identity verification is used. These include:

1. A verification code texted or emailed to your mobile phone that you must enter separately.
2. Digital fingerprints.
3. Facial recognition.
4. Iris scans.
5. A set of security questions that only you know.

If you do online banking, your bank is responsible for ensuring that this kind of multi-factor authentication is on your account because regulations require it.

More About Multi-Factor Authentication

- Don't use the same password on multiple accounts.
- Don't use the same security questions and answers on multiple accounts.
- Write them down to help you remember them and keep them in a secure place.
- When an online account offers the extra security of sending a secondary six digit pin to your phone for you to use as part of the login process, sign up for that!
- Set alerts on your accounts where the option exists. You'll be notified if someone tries to access the account and fails.
- Pay attention to all alert notifications.

Step 7
Check Statements Regularly

Early detection greatly limits the extent of damage caused by a criminal, as well as the time and expense to recover from fraudulent activity.

Review <u>monthly</u>:

1. Every credit card statement. Look for charges you don't recognize. Don't assume that a small charge is inconsequential. A small charge is often a "test" for a much bigger charge or withdrawal later by a criminal.
2. Every banking statement.
3. Be sure to reconcile your bank statement to your records to catch small errors that could be "test" charges.

Consider real time notifications and alerts from your bank.

1. Each time your account is charged or changed, you should receive an alert to your phone or email.
2. Don't ignore alerts.

Follow-up on Preauthorization Alerts

Preauthorization alerts will appear such as:

- $150 for gas when you only put in $25 worth of gas and you pay at the pump.
- $1 for an online purchase that is significantly larger.
- Alerts may be genuine or signal trouble.
- Follow-up on any alert that seems odd as soon as you can.

Bottom line:

- Set your account to send you alerts in real time.
- Check your statements monthly when they arrive.

Step 8
Check for Your Exposure
on the Dark Web

The Dark Web is the online universe where, among other things, your personal sensitive data is stored, traded, bought and sold by unauthorized individuals. It requires special encryption and anonymizing software and some authorizations to use.

1. You cannot check for your own data there unless you have all the necessary tools and authorizations.
2. There are services offered by different companies that check for your data on the Dark Web.
3. Eliminating your information from the Dark Web, if it is there, may not be possible.
4. If you are exposed, your best strategy is vigilance and to take the steps in this book.
5. Free websites such as https://haveibeenpwned.com/ are helpful.

What Does a Credit Monitoring Service Do?

Generically, for a monthly fee, credit monitoring services automate a lot of the manual search and discovery for your sensitive personal information:

- Gather data about you to build a profile of accounts, emails, SSN, passport number.
- Use tools they have developed to monitor the Internet and Dark Web for any information about you.
- Notify you when information is found.
- Assist you with the recovery process if a case of identity theft is found.
- Offer you a level of coverage up to some dollar limit, for necessary legal follow-up and paperwork processing.

These services rely on credit bureaus to gather data. Lifelock uses Equifax, for example. IDShield relies on Experian.

Step 9
Pick Great Passwords

Weak passwords are very easy to break. Strong passwords are very easy to create.

1. Choose a favorite phrase such as "I love snowboarding." That would be a great passphrase to use for a website on winter sports, for example.
2. Use symbols and numbers as substitutes for some of the letters. You can choose any combination of substitutes, but try to be consistent so it becomes a "system" for you.
3. For example Ilovesnowboarding becomes !L0v3Sn0wB0@rd1ng!
4. Don't use the same password on multiple sites.

Password Dos and Don'ts

- Do use an address book or electronic encrypted password vault to organize complex passwords and passphrases.
- Do make your password relevant to the site for which it is used to help you remember.
- Do avoid completely random complicated passwords – they are too hard to get right and could lock you out of your account.
- Do change your password if you suspect someone else knows it.
- Don't share passwords.
- Don't save any passwords on shared or public computers.

Step 10
Keep Your Sensitive Information Safe

1. Do not give your account information to family members or friends.
2. Do not use public computers to do sensitive business (like an online purchase) or login to accounts.
3. Do not use free, open WIFI for sensitive business.
4. Do not synch your phone to the onboard system in a rental car.
5. Do not allow friends to log in to your computer, laptop or phone.
6. Be careful of shoulder surfing when you enter your PIN on a keyboard.
7. Don't send account information to anyone by email or text.
8. Limit the use of your SSN as an identifier.
9. If someone asks you for your SSN, question if it is absolutely necessary.

Sharing Your Login Could Be Trouble

DO NOT SHARE YOUR PERSONAL ACCOUNTS

- Your personal accounts MUST be one person, one account.
- If any action happens on the account you don't recognize, you'll have an easier time tracking it down to a perpetrator.
- You'll know where your data is going – no accidental exports of files via email or file sharing.
- You can more easily defend any accusations of bad things happening with your computer when you know it was just you.

Step 11
Use a Shredder

Shredders are an essential appliance in every household. They should be used to securely dispose of anything containing PII. Personally Identifiable Information (PII) for the purpose of this discussion is anything that could be used to specifically identify an individual and could result in harm if that information were disclosed to the wrong people.

Examples:

You should shred any paper on which any of the following kinds of information is printed, instead of throwing it in the trash or recycle bin intact:

1. Bank statements
2. Utility bills
3. Credit card statements
4. Sensitive emails
5. Medical records
6. Printouts of bank registers
7. Drafts of tax paperwork
8. Tax filings you no longer need as records
9. Telephone records showing call details
10. Anything with your name and address on it

Options For Shredding

- A home shredder can be a cross-cut or micro shredder so that the paper is in little rectangles (or smaller), not long strips with readable information.
- For home, consider a heavy duty/high capacity version that will shred multiple sheets of paper, staples, CD/DVDs and credit cards.
- When in doubt, shred. You can recycle it just the same as non-shredded recyclable paper.
- For bulk shredding, check the local community resources for on-site shredding that will either come to your location (mobile unit), or is located nearby.
- Do not give your papers to someone else to "shred for you."

Step 12
What to Do with Data Storage

Data storage – also known as "Data at Rest," can be an easy target to get to a repository of your sensitive personal information by a criminal or snoop.

1. It is possible to retrieve data off of data storage devices unless they are encrypted or securely "wiped." Wiping is used when storage devices are going to be discarded or exchanged.
2. If you have a lot of data on a hard drive and it has crashed, it is best to not take the computer to the shop and leave it with the hard drive inside. Take it out and keep it safe at home.
3. Never give away a computer with an unencrypted hard drive inside without wiping all the data first.
4. Data storage devices you may use at home or in the office include:
    a. Internal hard drives
    b. External hard drives
    c. USB sticks
    d. RAID arrays
    e. External backup drives
    f. CDs/DVDs

Ways to Protect Your Data on Storage Devices

There are several tools and techniques to protect your data. Use Google search to find a technique for your specific device (e.g. "wipe USB.") They are:

- Full volume encryption
- File encryption
- Secure overwrite of entire drive
- Heavy ball pein hammer
- Magnetic bulk disk eraser
- Drill press holes through the drive

NOTE: Using "delete" does not remove data from the drive. It can be retrieved and read if it is not encrypted.

Step 13
Beware of Bogus Emails/Texts

Bogus emails, texts, and other social media fall into a general category of identity theft techniques called "Phishing." Phishers try to deceive you into disclosing sensitive information with emails that look official, but collect information from you and send it to criminals. Phishing is a very popular technique used by hackers to trick you.

Tips to spot Phishing attempts:

1. The official looking email, text, or social media post usually, but not always, has spelling and grammatical errors.
2. It will often use a well-recognized, respectable brand or company name like iTunes or Bank of America.
3. The email may ask you to click on a hyperlink embedded in the email.
4. The email creates a sense of urgency, either by giving you a problem, or a very short time frame, or both.
5. You will be asked to disclose information such as account login and password, bank account information, or other personal sensitive information.

Tips to Prevent Phishing Attacks from Stealing Your Data

- Carefully preview email in the preview screen.
- Never click on links inside an email even if you think it is trustworthy.
- If an unexpected email with an embedded link or attachment arrives from a friend, call them to confirm it is legitimate before opening anything.
- Never respond to emails asking you to provided sensitive personal information.
- Do not click on invitations in social media from people you do not know.
- If someone sends you a graphic or picture file embedded in an email, and you didn't expect it, don't click on it.
- Keep all your devices current with operating system and app updates and patches.
- Use a firewall on your computer and laptop and keep it in active mode.
- Always use updated anti-malware running on your computer.

Step 14
Open WIFI

Open WIFI is a local area network that does not use encryption to protect your information. On open WIFI, anyone with a network sniffer can read all the data you transmit, including User IDs and passwords.

Open WIFI is common in places such as:

1. Airports
2. Coffee Shops
3. Libraries
4. Rental vacation homes
5. Hotels

Tips For WIFI

All WIFI has an SSID that is the "name" of the WIFI. Whoever sets up the WIFI can choose any name to make the network look "safe."

- Don't join a network unless you know it is legit.
- The list of SSID names for WIFI options on your computer should show a little "lock" icon if they are using security.
- Look for WIFI encryption like WPA and WPA2.
- Never use a wide-open WIFI.
- Consider using a personal hotspot provided by your wireless provider if you are frequently on the road.
- Always secure your home WIFI.

Step 15
Protect Your Children

Children are a huge target in the online world for financial crime because their credit history is pristine. They are also subject to too much screen time, predatory individuals and cyberbullying by peers.

1. Be protective of your child's SSN.
2. Safely store or shred all documents with children's sensitive personal information.
3. Regularly review any brokerage, custodial or savings accounts you have set up for your children to look for suspicious activity.
4. Be very open with your children that you will be controlling and monitoring their online activity.
5. Use parental controls if you allow your child online. Use router tools that block, filter and monitor their online use.
6. Do not allow your child to download their own apps.
7. Know exactly what games and apps they are using and consider limiting them.
8. If your child has a mobile device, consider making a rule that you will review it frequently in order to check for dangerous communications.
9. Talk to your children about online safety.

A Word About Cyberbullying

More than a third of kids who are online experience cyberbullying. Talk to them so communication channels are open and they can come to you if cyberbullying becomes an issue for them.

Here are some tips:

- Ignore cyberbullies. Engaging them is most likely to escalate the behavior.
- Blocking may be ineffective as they use multiple accounts to persist.
- Tell your child to come to you as soon as they experience bullying.
- Keep a record of bullying, especially repeat bullying:
  - Save posts and texts to your computer in case you need them for proof, or
  - Keep a paper record of events
- If the cyberbully is a classmate, notify the school of this behavior.

You've finished. Before you go…

<u>Tweet/share that you finished this book.</u>

Please star rate this book.

Reviews are solid gold to writers. Please take a few minutes to give us some itty bitty feedback.

ABOUT THE AUTHOR

Karen Worstell, MS, MA is a cybersecurity expert who was inspired to study cybersecurity while a computer science grad student after her professor encrypted a final exam. She had to use her kit of code-breaking tools – and the rest, as they say, is history.

Her work was initially in research at companies like Boeing and SRI Consulting to develop computing models for the emerging world of distributed computing and the Internet. She presented appeals for improving cybersecurity for the Internet alongside luminaries like Donn Parker, Peter Neumann, Rhonda MacLean, the late Howard Schmidt, Fred Thompson, and the Secretary General of Interpol in the early 2000s. Later she held leadership roles in cybersecurity for Bank of America, AT&T Wireless and Russell Investments.

Today she consults on cybersecurity talent, matching cybersecurity professionals to the companies who need them, and provides coaching masterminds and intensives that contribute to improved cybersecurity by increasing resilience in IT pros in highly stressful roles.

She believes that computer science and cybersecurity are important career fields for everyone, and encourages women and young female students to excel as computer technology

33

professionals through her mentoring and coaching programs. She has spoken internationally on the topic of cybersecurity, is the author of books on the subject and is also a contributor to publications on cybersecurity, IT, and e-discovery.

If you liked this Itty Bitty® Book you might also enjoy:

- **Your Amazing Itty Bitty® Eldercare Book** – John Smith

- **Your Amazing Itty Bitty® Advanced Video Marketing Book** – Gary Howarth

- **Your Amazing Itty Bitty® Prospect-To-Profit Lead Generation Book** – Erin Smilkstein

Many more Itty Bitty® Books are available online.